THE BEVERAGE COOKBOOK

PREPARING FOOD THE HEALTHY WAY SERIES

THE BEVERAGE COOKBOOK

Frederick E. Kahn, M.D.
Edited by William Wright

Nautilus Communications, Inc.
New York, N.Y.

We wish to thank for their contributions and assistance the American Egg Board, American Dairy Association, United Dairy Industry Association, Pan American Coffee Bureau, Ocean Spray Company and Lipton Tea Company.

The publisher wishes to thank Scott Grayson and Andrea Spirn for their assistance in the preparation of this book.

Published by Nautilus Communications Inc.
460 East 79th Street, New York, N.Y. 10021

Design by Kathleen Cronin Tinkel

Cover illustration by Marilyn Ackerman

Printed in the United States of America

Contents

Preface

In recent years attention has been focused on the need for each of us to take control of our own future. The concept of self-help means that we should be able to choose how we act in various situations. One of those areas of choice is nutrition—the process or act of nourishing one's self. Furthermore, the changes in the way we feed ourselves have undergone a revolution.

In today's world, we spend time eating and making choices in ways that are very different from our ancestors. Before the use of cooking, people ate raw foods. Eventually, mankind discovered that cooking would change the taste of food. By the Roman times, emphasis was placed on the enjoyment of food as an activity, and as such, more attention was paid to its preparation. As our modes of transportation changed different cultures were introduced to foods from other areas of the world. Food preparation, however, remained laborious because of all the activities necessary to make food edible. Preservatives were primitive, at best, and packaging was not in use.

With the advent of industrialization, many changes occurred. First of all food could be transported rapidly over long distances. Refrigeration, packaging, and chemistry, allowed food to remain for prolonged periods of time on our shelves. Along with these changes, food preparation has also dramatically changed. Instead of using wood, we've moved to gas and electric methods of cooking, as well as using microwaves. Food preparation has speeded up in other areas with the advent of tools and machines to cut and process. Agricultural and technological advances have also added another dimension in producing healthier and more bountiful food stuffs.

The amount of time we have to spend on ourselves is quite different from what our grandparents had. Because of modern conveniences, along with changes in technology, we have much more leisure time. This allows much more time to follow pursuits other than working. Changes in structure of the family have also made us more isolated and the presence of a nuclear-style family, as well as increasing numbers of adult single individuals have promulgated feelings of loneliness. Food, being one of earliest contacts with our mothers along with feelings of warmth and wholeness, is a direction that we return to when feeling loneliness. Increasing influence of media has also made us focus much more on different brands of food as well as how and what we are eating. We are aware that we can do something to improve or prolong our lives through exercise and better nutrition.

Social changes have also played an important role in our changing notions of food—and eating. There have been dramatic alterations in the relationship of an individual to those around him or her. Family structure has changed, and where once the large, sprawling family units were the norm, we have now adopted the smaller, tightly-knit "nuclear family" style. There are also many more single adults who make up individual households. In both of these situations we are more likely to experience isolation and feelings of loneliness. Psychologists believe that eating is related to the feeling of warmth and security because of their association during infancy. We often eat when feeling lonely, to replace the lost sensation of wholeness that we experience as babies. When we feel this, we may eat too much or eat improperly.

The choice of what and how much food, where and when to eat, and why we are eating, along with an understanding of nutrition, help us develop the essentials of maintaining good health. Coronary heart disease, obesity, dental caries, iron deficiency anemia, and some types of emotional illnesses, result from a lack of attention to what we eat. You may significantly improve your health and increase your life span by being actively concerned about your nutritional intake.

This book will offer you a compendium that is directed toward healthier nutrition. It offers recipes which are designed to reduce excesses of food stuffs which may lead to poor health. It is not a prescription or formula. I take the attitude that there are many different ways to approach life, and as such, the same is true of our eating habits. Thus, this book presents one of those ways in which you can approach the preparation of food—a healthier way!

What you eat, and how you prepare it, is a decision left to each of you. It is your first step toward a more energetic and healthy life.

Frederick E. Kahn, M.D.

Beverages

Beverages

We are pleased to bring you this unique volume in our series and believe you will enjoy and profit from it enormously. There are virtually no comprehensive cookbooks on beverages alone, yet drinks are so much a part of our diet that they are almost taken for granted. We grow up hearing that a balanced diet contains at least eight glasses of liquid a day; this eight-glass standard covers a wide range of choices. In fact, no area of culinary preparation provides such a vast diversity as beverages.

Drinks in their diversity satisfy nearly every taste and occasion. From a party to a sick room, there is a beverage which will satisfy. There are drinks for diet conscious people, high calorie supplements for weight gain; there are times in hospital or after a visit to the dentist when only drinks are allowed. Many people have problems with high fiber digestion but need the nutrition in vegetables or fruit—juice is an answer. There are beverages for any climate or temperature or time of day.

Besides being so diverse, drinks are probably the simplest things to prepare in the kitchen. There is no recipe in this volume that takes longer to make than the time it takes coffee to perk or a juicer to extract the liquid from a bunch of carrots. For this reason we feel that you will enjoy this book of simple-to-make recipes.

We have left out alcoholic drinks as they are an area all their own. Many people do not drink and those who do are able to find a superfluity of recipes from the makers and distributors of liquor and wines. Many of the recipes here, however, can be the basis for an alcoholic beverage and if you are inclined to try the addition, feel free.

Actually, one of the purposes of our present volume is to encourage experiment. We have included as many drink recipes and ideas as we could think of but we hope that your creativity will be sparked and you'll go on to improve on, and perhaps invent your own beverage favorites.

We have categorized the book into seven chapters. They are sections dealing with egg-based drinks, milk and yogurt-based drinks, ice cream and sherbet shakes, fruit juice and punch combinations, vegetable juices, tea, and coffee combinations. As we go along, we offer some helpful hints on making yogurt and buttermilk, on finding the proper juice extractor, interesting information on the origin of tea and coffee and proper methods of brewing.

When you read through these recipes, you may come upon a favorite or one your tastebuds tell you to try. If you wish to halve the recipe, or extend it for a larger number, there is no recipe which cannot be adapted. Feel free to experiment, there may be some additional ingredient we hadn't thought of which will make the delicious beverage sublime. Good sipping and healthful drinking!

WEIGHTS AND MEASURES

dash – slightly less than ¼ teaspoon
3 teaspoons – 1 tablespoon
2 tablespoons – ⅛ cup – 1 ounce
4 tablespoons – ¼ cup – 2 ounces
5⅓ tablespoons – ⅓ cup
8 tablespoons – ½ cup – 4 ounces
10⅔ tablespoons – ⅔ cup
2 cups – 1 pint – ½ quart – 1 pound
4 cups – 2 pints – 1 quart
4 quarts – 1 gallon
8 dry quarts – 1 peck
4 pecks – 1 bushel

CAN SIZES

8 ounces – 1 cup
12 ounces – 1½ cup
1 pound or 16 ounces – 2 cups
20 ounces – 2½ cups

ABBREVIATIONS

c. – cup(s)
env – envelope(s)
F. – Fahrenheit
gal. – gallon(s)
in. – inch(es)
med. – medium
min. – minute(s)
oz. – ounce(s)
pkg. – package(s)
pt. – pint(s)
lb. – pound(s)
qt. – quart(s)
sec. – second(s)
T. – tablespoon(s)
t. – teaspoon(s)

Egg drinks

Egg drinks

The egg is the most nearly perfect protein available and also low in calories. It makes an ideal breakfast drink when blended with milk, fruit or vegetable juice. Many people do not care for eggs on a plate but find them palatable mixed in beverages; many people in our fast-paced culture do not have time to prepare a full breakfast but can spare two minutes to whirl a breakfast drink in the blender. For these groups we offer our egg drinks.

We tend to think of egg-based beverages as breakfast drinks only. They can be drunk at anytime; nutrition doesn't have to be considered only at breakfast. We recommend these drinks, too, for people who want to have less fat in their diet or who need to digest their meal more quickly; eggs cooked on the stove usually require butter or oil in preparation and this means added calories and added time in digestion. Athletes, dancers, people doing cardio-vascular intensive work need the nutrition of eggs but not necessarily the bolus of food in the stomach that a solid breakfast gives.

We stress again your own experimenting with the recipes here. Depending on your nutritional desires, you can add things like malt (for weight gain), wheat germ (for fiber bulk), brewer's yeast (for B vitamins), or fresh fruit (for vitamins and minerals).

Instant egg pickup

In the morning, this quick concoction provides needed nourishment to see you through till lunch. It's also great for a nightcap, or whenever an energy lift is needed.

1 egg
1 c. orange juice
1 T. honey, optional

Measure all ingredients into blender or shaker container. Cover. Blend or shake until well blended. Pour into tall glass. Serve immediately.

Serves 1.

Peptail

1 egg
½ c. milk
½ c. orange juice

Combine all ingredients; beat or shake until well blended. Pour into tall glass.

Serves 1.

Natural breakfast nog

1 egg
1 c. milk
1 T. honey, molasses or sugar
1 t. vanilla, optional
nutmeg or cinnamon, optional

Combine all ingredients; beat or shake until well blended. Pour into tall glass. Garnish with nutmeg, if desired.

Variation: For a breakfast egg shake, add scoop of vanilla, chocolate or strawberry ice cream; beat or blend until thick and frothy.

Serves 1.

Banana breakfast soda

1 egg
1 c. milk
1 small ripe banana, sliced
1 T. honey
1 scoop vanilla ice cream

Combine egg, milk, banana and honey; beat or blend until well blended. Pour into tall glass; top with ice cream.

Serves 1.

Tropic nog

1 egg
1 c. milk
2 T. frozen orange juice concentrate

Combine all ingredients; beat or blend until well blended. Pour into tall glass.

Serves 1.

Coffee cackle

1 egg
1 c. milk
1 T. maple-flavored syrup
1 t. instant coffee

Combine all ingredients; beat or shake until well blended. Pour into tall glass.

Serves 1.

Eye opener

1 egg
1 c. tomato juice
⅛ t. salt
⅛ t. Worcestershire sauce
dash Tabasco sauce

Combine all ingredients; beat with fork just until thoroughly combined. Pour into tall glass.

Serves 1.

Apple side up

1 egg
¾ c. apple juice
¼ c. milk
1 t. honey
¼ t. cinnamon

Combine all ingredients; beat or shake until well blended. Pour into tall glass.

Serves 1.

Breakfast fruit nog

1 egg
1 c. apricot, apple or prune juice

Combine egg and fruit juice; beat or shake until well blended. Pour into tall glass.

Serves 1.

Fruit 'n eggnog mix-up

3 eggs, slightly beaten
¼ c. sugar
⅛ t. salt
2 c. milk
½ t. vanilla

Mix eggs, sugar and salt together until well blended. Gradually stir in milk. Cook in heavy saucepan over medium heat, stirring constantly, until mixture thickens and just coats a spoon. Stir in vanilla. Pour into bowl or pitcher, cover and refrigerate several hours or overnight. To serve mix-ups, pour approximately ¾ cup eggnog mix-up into a tall glass. Stir in ½ cup apple, orange, grapefruit or cranberry juice.

Serves 2-3.

Banana eggnog

½ ripe banana
1 large egg
2 t. sugar, optional
¾ c. milk
nutmeg

Beat banana until smooth in a small mixing bowl. Add egg and sugar and beat thoroughly. Gradually add milk, beating until frothy. Serve sprinkled with nutmeg.

Serves 1.

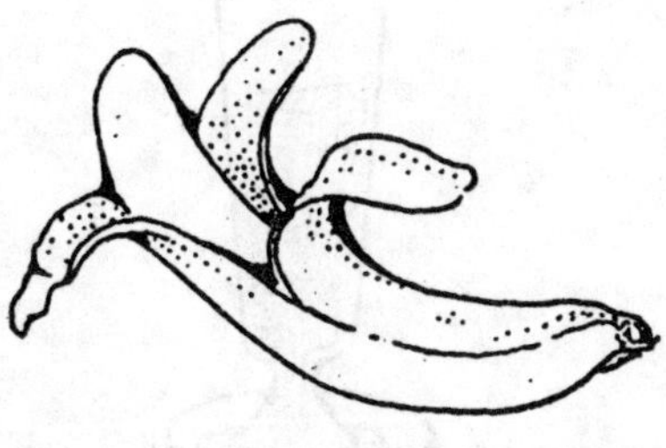

Egg cream

This drink evolved around the turn of the century on New York's lower east side. It was considered especially good for children, as it contains milk and eggs. Grownups like it too, and sometimes add a touch of spirits.

2 eggs
¾ c. milk
1 t. powdered coffee
2 T. chocolate syrup
1 c. club soda

Measure all ingredients except club soda into blender container. Cover and blend 20 seconds. Divide mixture between two 12 ounce glasses. Pour ½ cup club soda into each glass, stirring briskly to create a head of foam. Serve immediately.

Serves 2.

Egg sherbet

1 egg
1 c. orange juice
1 T. honey, optional
1 scoop orange or lemon sherbet

Combine egg, juice and honey, if desired; beat or shake until well blended. Pour into tall glass. Just before serving add a scoop of orange or lemon sherbet.

Serves 1.

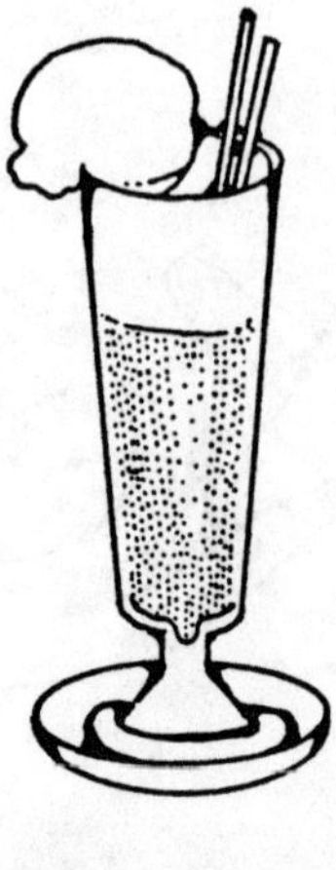

Here are some hearty nog punches which are filling and nourishing. Traditionally, nogs are served during the colder months, but we feel they are a festive treat welcome at any time.

Punchbowl eggnog

This frothy mixture of eggs, milk, rum and sugar was the customary drink of American colonists before setting out on a journey. It's still popular, and has a special place in holiday festivities.

6 eggs, slightly beaten
1 qt. milk
¼ c. sugar
¼ t. salt
1 c. whipping cream, whipped
rum or brandy flavoring
1 t. vanilla
nutmeg, optional

Blend together eggs, milk, sugar and salt. Fold in whipped cream, flavoring and vanilla. Pour into bowl or pitcher. Cover and refrigerate until thoroughly chilled, several hours or overnight. Sprinkle each serving with nutmeg, if desired.

Serves 6-8.

Spizzerinktum

6 eggs, slightly beaten
4½ c. chilled cranberry juice
1½ c. chilled orange juice
⅔ c. honey
⅓ c. lemon juice
orange and lemon slices, optional

Combine first 5 ingredients; beat well until thoroughly blended. Pour into punch bowl. Garnish with orange and lemon slices, if desired.

Serves 10-15.

Gold strike punch

6 eggs, slightly beaten
6 c. chilled orange juice
⅓ c. honey, optional
orange or lemon sherbet

Combine eggs, juice and honey, if desired; beat well until thoroughly blended. Pour into punch bowl. Add scoops of sherbet.

Serves 10-15.

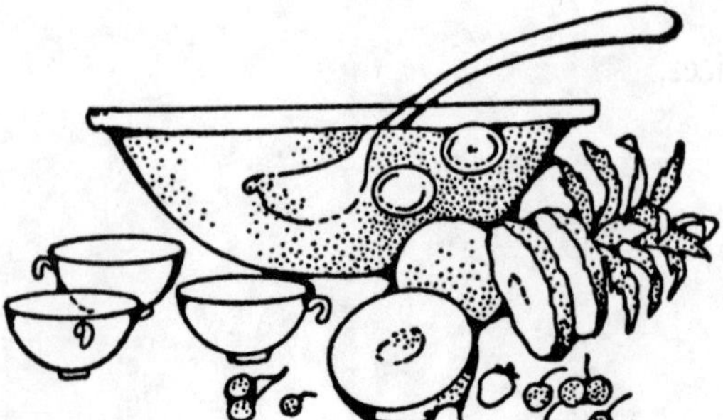

Milk drinks

Milk drinks

Milk-based drinks are almost limitless. Whether you choose whole milk, skimmed or non-fat powdered milk, buttermilk or yogurt, milk mixes with a variety of fruits and flavorings and spices. Many parents find that children who are not keen for plain milk love it flavored. The addition of a tablespoon of sugar and a dash of cinnamon makes a "shake" out of ordinary milk. An egg blended into this gives added protein to children who dislike cooked eggs.

We recommend using non-fat powdered milk in many of the following drinks. Non-fat is absolutely equal in protein to liquid milk and is cheaper, a consideration in a large family budget, and is essential in a reduced-calorie or low cholesterol diet. Of course, non-fat milk does not taste quite like fresh milk. For this reason consider trying it with the following recipes. Every box of non-fat dry milk solids has instructions on making the liquid milk equivalent. This can be used in the same proportion as milk called for in any recipe.

We have included a recipe for yogurt and buttermilk among our beverages because they are so nourishing and mix well with so many things. Buttermilk and yogurt share the quality of fermentation. Lactose, or milk sugar, is present in all milk. When lactobacilli are added to liquid milk, they multiply and digest this milk sugar, leaving as a byproduct lactic acid. This accounts for the slightly sour taste and thickening in buttermilk and yogurt. This process has been known for hundreds of years and was used as a means of keeping milk edible for longer periods.

The process has an added advantage. Many people when they reach adulthood are not able to digest lactose and this causes severe gastric upset. These people can, however, tolerate lactic acid and, consequently, can eat buttermilk and yogurt.

Many doctors recommend eating yogurt after a treatment of antibiotics. Many drugs kill off not only invading bacteria but also beneficial organisms which live in the human system and aid digestion. The consuming of lactobacilli is thought to reintroduce these needed helpful bacteria.

Making yogurt. Making yogurt at home is easy and inexpensive. It can be done for a quarter of the price of yogurt in the store. There are a variety of machines (about $25) which hold the yogurt mixture and keep it at the proper temperature of 104° F. while the culture incubates. All the machines are satisfactory. Some hold a one or two quart unit, others use five or six individual cups. Choose the machine which suits your needs, whether you need small portions or a large amount. The quart-sized unit for one or two people is not ideal since yogurt "bleeds" its water content when only used partially. When buying a machine with individual cups, avoid ones with hard-to-reach ridges or small mouths. Emptying yogurt from them can be a nuisance.

One can make yogurt without a commercial machine. Simply use a quart jar or individual glasses well-covered and placed near a warm radiator, a pilot light or in a warm-water bath in a slightly warm oven. We recommend machines over this crude method because the temperature is constant with them and yogurt takes eight to twelve hours to cure; temperature fluctuations are too problematic with ovens and radiators.

Yogurt can be made from whole milk or non-fat milk solids. The first gives a smoother, creamier yogurt because of the fat content, the latter gives a "chalkier," drier taste. Many older recipes required sterilizing the milk before adding the yogurt culture—a process which put most people off making yogurt altogether. That is not necessary today, unless you are using raw milk, directly from the farm. Milk in the store or milk solids have been pasteurized and are free from bacteria. If you are using raw milk, however, heat the milk to 140-160° F. and then allow the milk to cool to about 106° F. before adding the culture.

Most recipes make one quart of yogurt. If you start with one quart of liquid milk, add one cup of milk solids to it. If you are using only milk solids, double the amount of dry milk to be added to the water amount. This will make firm yogurt. Without the extra milk solids the yogurt will be watery and loose.

Many people like a solider product and get that by dissolving a packet of unflavored gelatin in ¼ cup of hot water and adding this to the yogurt mixture just before incubation.

After you have the milk mixture ready (with gelatin, if you wish), stir in approximately two tablespoons of yogurt. Make sure it is dissolved and distributed well. Health stores sell the lactobacillus culture in dry form and charge a great deal. We have used plain yogurt from grocery stores for years. Buy a small carton and use it for your cultures up to the date of freshness stamped on the carton. The best cultures are those which are not solidified with gelatin. You may be able to use yogurt beyond its freshness date, but the culture does weaken and may not give as good a finished product. The yogurt culture can also be used in your preparation of buttermilk. It is the same bacteria (*lactobacillus bulgaricus*) used in yogurt, buttermilk, sour cream, creme fraiche, clotted cream and cream cheese.

There are those who like the idea of yogurt but not its acidic taste. Sweetened yogurt is their preference. You can dissolve sugar in the mixture before incubation without problems. You can also add ½ teaspoon of your favorite flavoring as well. We have tried lemon, orange, almond, vanilla, maple and peppermint—all are delicious.

The yogurt culture will set in about eight hours. Many people, however, like a tangier, sharper taste and to get that the culture must cure longer. The yogurt will not be harmed even if left up to twenty-four hours. You must watch it though since it has a tendency to separate into curds and whey if left over-long. If this happens, it is not spoiled and can be blended in our beverage recipes as easily as softer yogurt.

Yogurt drink

½ c. grape juice
1 c. apple juice
2 T. yogurt
¼ c. raisins
dash cinnamon

Mix all ingredients in blender until smooth and creamy. Serve in wine glasses.

Serves 2.

Yogurt shake

1 c. yogurt
1 c. milk
4 ice cubes
1 ripe banana
6 pitted dates
2 T. honey
4 almonds

Mix all ingredients in blender for 2 min. and serve in chilled glasses.

Serves 2.

Frosty shake

¾ c. lemon flavored iced tea mix
2 c. (16 oz.) vanilla yogurt
1 can (6 oz.) frozen orange juice concentrate
2½ c. ice cubes (about 17 to 20)

In blender, combine all ingredients except ice cubes; process at high speed until blended. Add ice cubes, one at a time; process at high speed until blended.

Serves 5.

Breakfast fruit cocktail cocktail

1 can (17 oz.) fruit cocktail in juice
1 c. yogurt, plain
2 T. toasted wheat germ
1 t. brown sugar
1 t. vanilla
⅛ t. nutmeg

Combine fruit cocktail with all liquid and remaining ingredients in blender. Whirl smooth. Pour into glasses to serve.

Serves 3.

Cranberry grape yogurt shake

2 c. grape cranberry drink
1 c. frozen vanilla yogurt

In a blender container, process grape cranberry drink and yogurt on high until blended.

Serves 4.

Lemon yogurt pick-up

½ c. sliced fresh strawberries
1 T. sugar
1 c. (8 oz.) lemon yogurt
¾ c. milk
fresh strawberries

Beat strawberries and sugar in a blender until mashed. Add yogurt and milk. Blend just until foamy. Garnish with fresh strawberries, if desired. Serve immediately.

Serves 2.

Here are three yogurt drinks from India. Yogurt has been used in cooking and drinking there for centuries—a nutritious solution to scarce meat and a palate cooler for hot climates and spicy foods.

Dahi

1 qt. yogurt
juice of 12 limes or lemons
½ to 1 c. raw sugar or honey
3 qt. water

Place yogurt, lime juice and sugar to taste in an electric blender and blend until sugar has dissolved.

Pour into a gallon jug or container and fill with ice cold spring water.

Serves 16.

Indian lassi

2 c. yogurt
4 c. water
¼ t. salt
½ t. cumin powder
pinch cayenne

Mix all ingredients in blender for 1 min. Chill well before serving.

Serves 8.

Tahn

1 c. yogurt
3 c. ice water
ice cubes
1 sprig fresh mint, optional

Combine yogurt and water and fresh mint in an electric blender and blend 1 min. Pour over ice cubes.

Serves 4.

Buttermilk

Buttermilk is really misnamed. It is made from the milk and whey mixed together after butter is whipped. The whey contains flecks of butter which one finds in buttermilk.

½ c. instant nonfat dry milk
1½ c. lukewarm water
¼ c. fresh buttermilk

Mix dry milk and water. Add buttermilk, cover and let stand at room temperature about 8 hours until thickened. Stir until smooth. Cover and chill.

Try keeping the developing buttermilk above the pilot light if you use a gas stove. This is about the right heat to keep the bacteria alive.

Serves 1.

Buttermilk smoothie

1 c. buttermilk
1 ripe banana, or peeled and seeded orange, apple, pear, etc.
1-2 t. sugar

Blend ingredients in mixer until smooth and frothy. Add a dash of cinnamon or nutmeg when serving.

Serves 1.

Orange breakfast bracer

3 T. frozen orange juice concentrate
1 t. honey
1 c. cold buttermilk
orange slice

Combine orange juice concentrate and honey. Add buttermilk. Beat with a mixer or a blender just until foamy. Garnish with orange slice, if desired. Serve immediately.

Serves 1.

Pineapple-orange buttermilk refresher

- 2 c. cold buttermilk
- ½ c. chilled unsweetened pineapple juice
- ½ c. chilled fresh orange juice
- 2 t. fresh lemon juice
- ¼ c. sugar
- pineapple and orange pieces

Place all ingredients, except pineapple and orange pieces, in blender container; cover. Blend until frothy and sugar is dissolved. Serve immediately in tall chilled glasses garnished with pineapple and orange pieces.

Serves 2.

Frosty buttermilk nog

- 3 c. buttermilk
- 1 can (8¼ oz.) crushed pineapple, chilled
- ¼ c. honey
- 1 t. vanilla
- ⅛ t. salt
- 4 ice cubes

Place all ingredients, except ice cubes, in blender container. Cover and blend. Add ice cubes, one at a time, blending until mixture is nearly smooth and frothy. Serve in chilled mugs.

Serves 3.

Simple banana milk shake

- 1 ripe banana
- 1 t. sugar
- 1 c. milk
- dash cinnamon
- ½ t. vanilla extract

Blend ingredients in mixer until smooth and frothy.

Serves 1.

Orange punch

5 c. cold water
1 c. nonfat dry milk
1 can (12 oz.) concentrated unsweetened orange juice

Mix water with milk powder and add concentrated juice. Stir well or blend. Chill.

Serves 5.

Fruit milk shake

3 c. ripe fresh fruit in season or canned fruit in light syrup or natural juice
½ c. nonfat dry milk
1 c. water or drained juice from can
8 ice cubes

Peel fruit if necessary. Cut fruit into pieces, and mash through a strainer or in a food mill. Crush ice cubes (one way is to place them in a heavy plastic bag and use a rolling pin or hammer.). Blend fruit, milk powder, and liquid with a beater. Add crushed ice and blend again.

Serves 4.

Orange strawberry wake-up

1 c. orange juice
1 c. fresh strawberries
1 egg
½ c. non-instant dry milk powder
½ c. water

Put all ingredients in an electric blender and blend until smooth.

Serves 4.

Papaya drink

½ c. papaya, peeled and seeded
2 t. sugar
½ c. milk
1 t. lemon juice

Whip ingredients in blender and serve in chilled glass. Variation: substitute mango, kiwi, guava or melon for a different tropical taste.

Serves 1.

Strawberry breakfast soda

1 egg
1 c. milk
1 T. strawberry preserves
1 scoop strawberry ice cream (optional)

Combine egg, milk and strawberry preserves; beat or shake until well blended. Pour into tall glass. Add ice cream.

Serves 1.

Cappy C.'s breakfast-in-a-glass

2 c. milk
1 scoop vanilla ice cream
1 egg
1 banana
1 T. brewer's yeast
2 T. high protein powder
3 T. wheat germ

Mix all ingredients in blender at high speed for 2 min.

Serves 1.

Fruit and milk flip

1 c. milk
6 ice cubes, crushed
1 T. honey
¾ c. diced mixed fresh fruits such as apples, strawberries, blueberries, pears, peaches and apricots.

Place all ingredients in an electric blender and blend 30 seconds.

Serves 2.

Orange shake

2 heaping t. orange powdered soft drink mix
1 c. cold milk
orange ice cubes*

Add drink mix to milk in glass or shaker. Stir or shake until dissolved. Add 1 or 2 orange ice cubes. Serve immediately.

*Orange ice cubes: Stir 4 heaping teaspoons of drink mix into 2 cups milk; stir until dissolved. Pour into 1 ice cube tray. Freeze until firm. To release ice cubes, dip bottom of tray in warm water a few seconds. Store ice cubes in a tightly sealed plastic bag in freezer.

Serves 1.

Raspberry frosty

1 pkg. (10 oz.) frozen raspberries in syrup, thawed
1 pt. raspberry sherbet
2 c. cold milk

Beat raspberries and sherbet with a mixer or a blender. Add milk. Beat just until foamy. Serve immediately.

Serves 3.

Pineapple blender ade

½ c. cottage cheese
1 can (8 oz.) crushed pineapple in unsweetened juice, chilled
2 eggs
2 c. cold milk
dash salt

Beat cottage cheese, pineapple with juice and eggs in a blender. Add milk and salt. Blend just until foamy. Serve immediately.

Serves 4.

Chocolate steamer

4 c. milk
2 T. freeze-dried coffee
2 T. chocolate syrup
⅛ t. salt
½ t. vanilla extract
½ t. brandy extract

Combine milk, coffee, syrup and salt in a 2 quart saucepan. Heat to serving temperature. Add vanilla and brandy extracts. Serve topped with whipped cream and chocolate curls, if desired.

Serves 4.

Continental iced coffee swirl

2 T. instant coffee powder
2 T. sugar
½ c. water
4 c. cold milk
few drops peppermint extract
½ c. whipping cream
2 T. cold fudge topping for ice cream

Dissolve instant coffee and sugar in water. Add milk and peppermint extract. Cover and keep chilled until serving time. Whip cream in a chilled bowl with chilled beaters until stiff peaks form. Gently fold in topping just until swirled through whipped cream to give a marbled pattern. Serve a dollop of fudge marbled whipped cream over each cup of iced coffee.

Serves 6.

Tea 'n cocoa warmer

3 T. instant tea powder
⅓ c. sugar
3 T. unsweetened cocoa powder
¼ t. ground cinnamon
1 qt. milk

In large saucepan, combine instant tea powder, sugar, cocoa powder, cinnamon and ½ cup milk. Cook over medium heat, stirring constantly, 2 min. Stir in remaining milk; heat through, stirring occasionally. Garnish, if desired, with mini-marshmallows.

Serves 6.

Peanut banana cooler

1 small ripe banana, sliced
2 T. creamy peanut butter
1 T. honey
1 c. cold milk
banana slice
chopped peanuts

Set aside one slice of banana for garnish. Beat remaining banana, peanut butter and honey in a blender until smooth. Add milk. Blend just until foamy. Garnish with banana slice, rolled in chopped peanuts, if desired. Serve immediately.

Serves 1.

Peanut honey smoothie

¼ c. honey
¼ c. creamy peanut butter
3 c. cold milk
½ t. vanilla extract
ice cream, if desired

Place honey, peanut butter and ¼ cup milk in blender container; cover. Blend until smooth. Add remaining milk and vanilla. Blend until smooth and frothy. Serve immediately, garnished with a small scoop of ice cream.

Serves 6.

Blueberry yogurt cooler

3 c. cold milk
1 c. blueberry yogurt
1 c. fresh blueberries
1 T. sugar

Blend milk, yogurt, blueberries and sugar in blender. Pour into glasses. Garnish with fresh blueberries, if desired. Serve immediately.

Serves 3.

Apricot-pineapple milk punch

2 c. apricot nectar, chilled
1 c. pineapple juice, chilled
1 T. fresh lemon juice
3 pt. vanilla ice cream, softened
4 c. cold milk

Gradually add fruit juices to ice cream; stir until blended. Stir in milk. Chill. Serve with fruit and mint-filled milk cubes. To make fruit and mint-filled cubes, pour a small amount of milk into bottom of ice cube tray. Place an apricot half or a pineapple chunk and a sprig of mint in milk; freeze until firm. Pour in milk to fill ice cube tray. Freeze several hours or overnight. This keeps punch cold and does not dilute the flavor with water.

Serves 12.

Summer punch

1 c. orange sherbet
1 c. milk
1 T. instant tea powder
½ c. pineapple juice
2 T. lemon juice
2 c. milk

In a large mixing bowl soften orange sherbet. In 1 cup milk dissolve tea powder; set aside. Blend pineapple and lemon juices into sherbet. Gradually blend in milk-tea mixture and remaining 2 cups milk. Serve immediately.

Serves 3

Milk party punch

½ c. powdered red punch drink mix
½ c. cold water
3 c. cold milk
milk ice cubes*

Pour drink mix into bowl; stir in water until dissolved. Pour milk into serving pitcher. Pour dissolved punch into milk, stirring constantly. Add milk ice cubes. Serve immediately.

*Milk ice cubes: Pour 2 cups milk into ice cube tray; freeze until firm. To release, dip bottom of tray in warm water a few seconds, turn out.

Serves 4.

Orange frosty

1 c. cold strong coffee
1 c. milk
1 c. orange juice
3 T. sugar

Mix all ingredients in blender at high speed. Garnish with orange slice.

Serves 3-4.

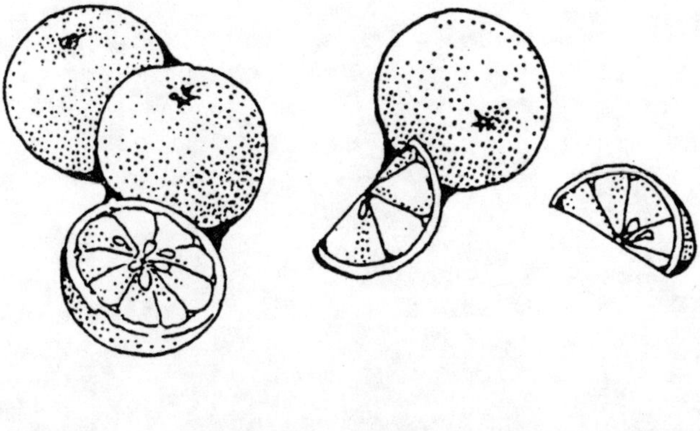

Ice cream shakes and sodas

Ice cream shakes and sodas

Ice cream is thought to have been created by the Romans, who kept a steady stream of slaves busy bringing snow down from the high mountains for this delicacy. What is better than ice cream or its milk-based brother, sherbet? Perhaps nothing except ice cream shakes and sodas, the nineteenth century's contribution to this dessert confection.

Shakes are basically ice cream plus a little milk and flavoring. The flavoring can be any kind of fresh fruit and one can use fruit juice instead of milk. Whatever your palate tells you will be tasty is a possible shake combination. Our recipes don't begin to cover all possibilities, but they give you a marvelous indication of what will please you and your guests.

Sodas are ice cream, flavoring and carbonated water (club soda or seltzer). They were so "sinfully" popular during the late 1800s and had so many people rushing to ice cream parlors directly from church, that the story has it the clergy had to take matters in hand. In several New England communities, ice cream sodas were prohibited on Sunday. As a result, ice cream sellers bent the law a bit and served only ice cream and topping without the soda, and called it a "sundae."

Malted milks should be included here, though we don't have any recipes for them. Malts are merely ice cream shakes plus a teaspoon of malt powder mixed in. Malt powder can be bought at any supermarket and added to any shake recipe you find in our volume. Malts have rather gone out of fashion today, perhaps because of the added calories, but they are distinct and delicious.

A final word about shakes and ice cream. Ice cream that has melted and been refrozen will be icy and unpleasant by itself. When blended into a shake, however, it tastes the same as fresh ice cream; don't discard old ice cream, use it in a tasty shake.

We feel that almost any good ice cream blends well into a shake or soda and very often it is as good to use a less expensive brand. Keep this in mind when serving a large amount. For fewer calories you may want to substitute frozen yogurt or ice milk. Ice milk, made from skimmed milk, contains the fewest calories. Frozen yogurt has the same as regular supermarket ice cream. Specialty ice creams contain the most because of their density and butter fat level.

High-cal/high protein shake

2 c. cold whole milk
1 scoop vanilla ice cream
1 banana
1 whole egg
2 T. honey
2 T. high protein powder
1 T. brewer's yeast
3 T. wheat germ

Place all ingredients in blender and whip for 3 min.

Serves 2.

Creamsicle shake

2 scoops vanilla ice cream
2 c. orange juice

Blend in blender until thick and creamy.

Serves 2.

Golden apricot shake

1½ c. apricot nectar, fresh or canned
1 c. milk
1 t. lemon juice
2 c. eggnog or vanilla ice cream
dash nutmeg

Put all ingredients in an electric blender and blend until smooth.

Serves 4.

Ambrosia shake

2 c. boiling water
6 almond herbal tea bags or
6 teabags plus 1 t. almond extract
¼ c. sugar
2 med. bananas
2 c. (1 pt.) vanilla ice cream
1½ c. ice cubes (about 9 to 11)
1 can (8 oz.) crushed pineapple in natural juice, drained
flaked coconut

In teapot, pour boiling water over almond herbal tea bags; cover and brew 5 min. Remove tea bags; stir in sugar and cool. In blender, combine tea, bananas and ice cream; process at high speed until blended. Add ice cubes, one at a time; process at high speed until blended. Top with pineapple, coconut and, if desired, additional ice cream.

Serves 4.

Banana shake

1½ c. cold strong coffee
3 T. sugar
1 banana
1 c. vanilla ice cream

Cut banana in chunks and combine with coffee and sugar in blender at high speed. When mixture is smooth add ice cream and blend at medium speed until smooth.

Serves 2.

Mocha frost

2½ c. cold coffee, extra strength
1 pt. coffee ice cream

Combine ingredients in bowl, blend with rotary beater until smooth Pour into tall glasses.

Serves 4.

Coffee nectar

2¼ c. cold coffee, extra strong
1 T. Angostura bitters
1 pt. coffee ice cream

Combine all ingredients in bowl and blend or beat until smooth and creamy. Pour into tall glasses.

Serves 3-4.

Rhubarb delight

1½ c. unsweetened pineapple juice, chilled
1 c. diced raw rhubarb
½ c. honey
1 pt. strawberry ice cream, softened

Place pineapple juice, rhubarb and honey in blender container; cover. Liquefy until almost smooth, about 1 min. Add ice cream. Blend until smooth and frothy. Serve immediately in tall chilled glasses.

Note: if fresh rhubarb is not available, the frozen unsweetened variety may be used. Use the same amount; let the fruit thaw slightly.

Serves 4.

Strawberry cooler

1 c. sliced fresh strawberries
2 T. honey
2 c. cold milk
1 pt. strawberry ice cream, softened

Place strawberries, honey and a small amount of milk in blender container; cover. Purée until almost smooth. Add remaining milk and ice cream. Blend until smooth and frothy, about 1 min. Serve immediately in tall chilled glasses garnished with a fresh whole strawberry.

Serves 4.

Banana cooler

2 med. bananas, sliced
2 T. honey
2 c. cold milk
1 pt. vanilla ice cream, softened
½ t. ginger

Place bananas, honey and a small amount of milk in blender container; cover. Purée until almost smooth. Add remaining milk, ice cream and ginger. Blend until smooth and frothy, about 1 min. Serve immediately in tall chilled glass garnished with a banana slice.

Serves 4.

Peach cooler

2 c. peeled chopped fresh peaches (about 3 med.)
3 T. honey
2¼ c. milk
1 pt. peach or vanilla ice cream, softened
¼ t. almond extract

Place peaches, honey and a small amount of milk in blender container; cover. Purée until almost smooth. Add remaining milk, ice cream and extract. Blend until smooth and frothy, about 1 min. Serve immediately in tall chilled glasses garnished with a fresh peach slice.

Serves 5.

Peach shake

1 pkg. (10 oz.) frozen sliced peaches in syrup, thawed
1 pt. vanilla or peach ice cream
2 c. cold milk
peach ice cream

Beat peaches and ice cream with a mixer or a blender. Add milk. Whip just until foamy. Top each serving with a scoop of ice cream, if desired. Serve immediately.

Serves 4.

Cherry vanilla punch

1 pt. vanilla ice cream
1 pkg. (3 oz.) cherry flavor gelatin
4 c. cold milk

Beat ice cream and gelatin with a mixer or a blender until smooth. Add 2 cups milk. Beat just until foamy. Add remaining milk. Serve at once.

Serves 6.

Chocolate orange milk whiz

3 c. cold chocolate milk
2 pt. orange sherbet
½ c. whipping cream, whipped
cinnamon

Beat 1 cup chocolate milk and 1 pint of sherbet with a mixer or a blender until smooth. Add remaining milk. Beat just until foamy. Top each serving with a scoop of remaining sherbet and a dollop of whipped cream. Sprinkle with cinnamon, if desired. Serve immediately.

Serves 4.

Chocolate peppermint milk shake

1 pt. vanilla ice cream
⅓ c. chocolate flavor milk mix
2 c. cold milk
dash peppermint extract
vanilla ice cream
crushed peppermint stick candy

Beat ice cream and milk mix with a mixer or a blender until smooth. Add milk and extract. Whip until foamy. Top each serving with a scoop of ice cream and sprinkle with candy, if desired. Serve immediately.

Serves 4.

Orange apricot shake

2½ c. cold milk
1 pt. orange sherbet, softened
½ c. dried apricots, chopped
2 T. sugar
½ t. vanilla extract

Place half the milk, half the sherbet, the apricots, sugar and vanilla in blender container; cover. Chop 1 min. Add remaining milk and sherbet. Blend until smooth and frothy. Serve immediately in tall chilled glasses.

Serves 4.

Kona coffee punch

1 c. cold coffee
1 c. tropical fruit punch
1 c. vanilla ice cream

Mix all ingredients in blender at high speed. Serve in punch glasses.

Serves 3-4.

Cherry chiller

1 c. cold strong coffee
1½ c. cherry ice cream
2 T. maraschino cherry juice, optional

Mix in blender at medium speed. Serve in "on-the-rocks" glasses.

Serves 2-3.

Café Hawaiian

2 c. cold strong coffee
1 c. chilled pineapple juice
2 T. sugar
2 c. coffee ice cream

Combine ingredients and beat with rotary beater or in blender until smooth and foamy. Pour into tall glasses.

Serves 4.

Icy lemon coffee

2 c. cold strong coffee
2 c. lemon sherbet
1 oz. grenadine syrup

Mix in blender at medium speed. Serve in slender glasses.

Serves 4.

Café chocomalt

1 c. cold strong cofee
1 c. milk
1 c. chocolate ice cream
2 T. sugar
3 T. malted milk powder

Mix all ingredients in blender at high speed. Serve in tall glasses.

Serves 2.

Viennese velvet

4 c. cold strong coffee
4 c. vanilla ice cream
1 c. whipped cream

Alternate coffee and scoops of ice cream in 6 parfait glasses. Top with whipped cream.

Serves 6.

Raspberry coffee shake

1 c. cold strong coffee
1½ c. raspberry ice cream or sherbet

Mix in blender at medium speed. Serve in tall glasses with orange slice.

Serves 2.

Mocha velvet

Fill tall glasses to brim with alternating scoops of chocolate, coffee and vanilla ice cream. Pour strong, hot coffee into the glasses and top each one with whipped cream. You'll spoon this satiny-smooth cooler at the beginning, but you'll end up by sipping through a straw.

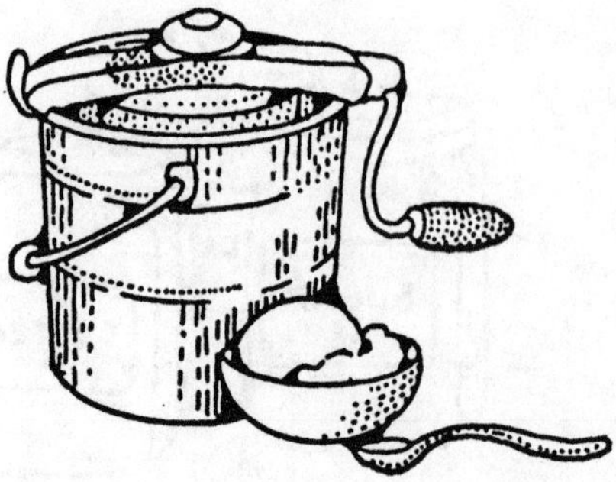

Mocha frosted

2½ c. strong, cold coffee
1 pt. coffee ice cream
5 T. chocolate syrup

Place all ingredients in bowl and blend with rotary beater until smooth. Pour into tall glasses.

Serves 4.

Banana coffee batido

2 ripe bananas
½ pt. (1 c.) coffee ice cream
½ c. light cream
¼ t. almond extract
1 T. instant coffee powder
½ t. lemon juice
1 T. sugar

Slice bananas into electric blender. Add ice cream, light cream, almond extract, coffee powder, lemon juice and sugar. Blend until thick and fluffy. Pour into 2 tall glasses. Serve at once, or chill until ready to serve.

Serves 2.

Coffee frosted

½ c. instant non-fat dry milk powder
½ c. ice water
¼ c. sugar
2 T. instant coffee powder
1 pt. coffee ice cream, slightly softened

Chill beater blades and small bowl of electric mixer. Measure instant dry milk into chilled bowl. Add ice water; blend. Beat at high speed until soft peaks form (about 5 min.). Combine sugar and instant coffee. Add slowly, continuing to beat. Turn to low speed. Add ice cream, about a quarter of it at a time, beating after each addition until blended. Serve at once.

Serves 3-4.

Cranberry scoop

1 c. cranberry juice cocktail
8 fresh or frozen whole strawberries
½ banana, sliced
½ c. vanilla frozen yogurt (or ice cream)

In a blender container, process cranberry juice cocktail, strawberries, banana, and frozen yogurt on high until smooth.

Serves 4.

Grapefruit pineapple shake

2 c. grapefruit juice, chilled
1 can (8 oz.) crushed pineapple, packed in its own juice
1½ c. vanilla ice cream

In a blender container, process grapefruit juice, pineapple, and ice cream until smooth and frothy.

Serves 6-8.

Maple milk shake

2 c. cold milk
1 pt. (2 c.) vanilla ice cream, softened
½ c. maple syrup

Place all ingredients in blender container; cover. Blend until smooth and frothy. Serve immediately in tall chilled glasses.

Serves 4.

Frosty apple cow

2 c. cold milk
1 pt. vanilla ice cream, softened
1 can (6 oz.) frozen concentrated apple juice
¼ t. cinnamon, nutmeg

Place all ingredients in blender container; cover. Blend until smooth and frothy. Serve immediately in tall chilled glasses.

Serves 4.

Mixed fruit drink

1 can (16 oz.) fruit cocktail in unsweetened juice, chilled
1 pt. vanilla ice cream, softened
1 c. cold milk

Place fruit and juice, ice cream and milk in blender container; cover. Blend until smooth and frothy. Serve immediately in tall chilled glasses.

Serves 4.

Orange-berry cooler

1 c. cold strong coffee
1 c. orange juice
2 c. strawberry ice cream
2 T. sugar

Mix all ingredients in blender at high speed. Serve in tall glasses.

Serves 2-3.

Purple cow milk punch

½ pt. vanilla ice cream
1 can (6 oz.) frozen concentrated grape juice
1 env. vanilla instant breakfast
2 c. milk
2 T. lemon or lime juice
vanilla ice cream or sweetened whipped cream

In a mixing bowl or blender beat ice cream; add grape juice and instant breakfast. Add milk and lemon juice. Pour into glasses. Top each with a small scoop of ice cream or sweetened whipped cream, if desired.

Serves 4.

Pineapple orange frosty

2 c. cold milk
1 pt. pineapple sherbet, softened
2 seedless oranges, peeled and quartered
2 T. sugar

Place half the milk, half the sherbet, the oranges and sugar in blender container; cover. Blend until almost smooth. Add remaining milk and sherbet. Blend until smooth and frothy. Serve immediately in tall chilled glasses.

Serves 3.

Cherry vanilla shake

2 pt. vanilla ice cream, softened
1 pkg. (3 oz.) cherry flavor gelatin
4 c. cold milk

Beat ice cream and gelatin with a mixer or a blender until smooth. Add 2 cups milk. Beat just until foamy. Add remaining milk. Serve at once.

Serves 6.

Orangy milk punch

1 qt. vanilla ice cream
2 pt. orange sherbet
1 bottle (16 oz.) carbonated lemon-lime beverage
1 qt. milk

Combine softened ice cream and sherbet and lemon-lime beverage; chill. Before serving, gradually add milk; beat until mixture is smooth. Serve in punch bowl. Garnish with orange slices, if desired.

Serves 15-20.

Buttermilk strawberry punch

1 qt. cold buttermilk
1 pt. strawberry ice cream
¼ c. confectioner's sugar

Beat all ingredients with rotary blender until blended. Serve garnished with whole strawberries.

Serves 15-20.

New York special milk punch

1½ qt. vanilla ice cream, softened
3 c. chilled pineapple juice
½ c. orange juice
1 T. lemon juice
1 qt. fresh cold milk

Add all ingredients in a large bowl and beat until frothy. Pour into a chilled punch bowl.

Serves 20-25.

Lemon tea refresher

1 pt. lemon sherbet, softened
⅓ c. instant tea powder
2 T. sugar
3 c. cold milk
lemon slices

Beat sherbet, instant tea and sugar with a mixer or blender until smooth. Add milk. Beat just until foamy. Garnish with lemon slices, if desired. Serve immediately.

Serves 4.

Frosty apple health drink

1 gal. fresh cold milk
1 can (12 oz.) apple concentrate
1½ qt. vanilla ice cream, softened
cinnamon
nutmeg

Add all ingredients in a large bowl and beat until frothy. Pour into a chilled punch bowl. Add cinnamon and nutmeg to taste.

Serves 20-25.

Kitty Bob's orange soda

1½ c. orange juice
¾ c. seltzer or club soda
2 scoops of vanilla ice cream

Place orange juice in 2 large, tall glasses and add seltzer or club soda. Top with scoop of vanilla ice cream.

Serves 2.

Pink grapefruit cranberry frosty

1 c. pink grapefruit juice cocktail
1 c. cranberry juice cocktail
½ c. lemon sherbet

In a blender, whip pink grapefruit juice cocktail, cranberry juice cocktail and sherbet until blended.

Serves 4.

Cranberry grape soda

1 c. grape cranberry drink
2 scoops strawberry ice cream
fruit flavored soda (dietetic, if desired)

In a blender container, process grape cranberry drink and 1 scoop ice cream until smooth. Pour into glass with remaining ice cream. Top with soda.

Serves 1.

Black cow soda

6 oz. root beer, chilled
3 small scoops (¾ c.) vanilla ice cream
chilled club soda or seltzer

Fill a 14-ounce glass ⅓ full with root beer. Add 1 scoop ice cream. Pour in about ¼ cup more root beer. Add 2 more scoops of ice cream. Pour in enough root beer to fill glass. Serve with club soda to add for extra carbonation, if desired.

Serves 2

Strawberry soda

3 T. frozen strawberries in syrup, thawed
3 small scoops (¾ c. strawberry ice cream)
6 oz. chilled creme soda
whipped cream
fresh strawberry

Mash strawberries until well blended with syrup. Stir together strawberry syrup, 1 scoop ice cream and about 2 tablespoons creme soda in the bottom of a 14 ounce glass. Add 2 additional scoops of ice cream. Pour in enough soda to fill glass. Garnish with whipped cream and a strawberry.

Serves 2.

Ski-lodge nog

1 c. water
6 cinnamon flavor tea bags
3 c. milk
½ c. maple syrup
¼ t. ground allspice
vanilla ice cream

In medium saucepan, bring water to a boil. Add cinnamon flavor tea bags; cover and brew 5 min. Remove tea bags. Stir in milk, maple syrup and allspice; heat through. Just before serving, top with ice cream.

Serves 8.

Fruit juices and punches

Fruit juices and punches

Nothing is more thirst quenching and energy building than fruit juice. There are so many kinds to try, but we tend to get in a rut and think only of the standard morning glass of orange juice, or, occasionally, apple cider or grapefruit juice. Next time you are shopping, consider the variety in the frozen concentrate section or on the canned juice shelf. Also consider how delicious the combination of two different juices might be. The tartness of cranberry or grape or grapefruit juice doesn't need additional sugar if you find it too sharp; mix in naturally sweet apple juice or the smooth nectar from pears, papayas, or mangos. Some people find nectars too thick, but an equal part of club soda or a thinner juice might make nectar quite drinkable to them.

Consider the addition of coconut milk to your favorite fruit drink. The smooth, creamy milk turns almost any juice into a tropical wonder.

Almost any juice can become a party punch by adding a scoop of sherbet with a complementary flavor and garnishing with a slice of orange, lemon or lime.

With the benefit of a blender, any fruit, berry, melon can be whirred into a frothy and refreshing drink by adding fruit juice, milk, ice cubes, club soda, ice cream or combination. There are several spices, too, which will add a delicious bouquet to your created fresh-fruit drinks: try a dash of cinnamon, cloves, nutmeg, mace, or ginger with a little of your drink to see which complements it the best.

Very often, fruit which is in season will be cheaper when blended in a drink than buying the same fruit as juice in concentrate or in can. Fruit is also more nutritious when fresh and blended into juices in its entirety. Remember that fruit which may be too ripe to eat can be blended into delicious drinks with no loss in flavor.

Lemonade/Limeade

grated rind of 6 lemons (or limes)
juice of 12 lemons (or limes)
2 qt. boiling water
2¼ c. sugar
cold water
ice cubes

Combine the rind and juice and let stand overnight. Pour the boiling water over the sugar, stir to dissolve, bring to a boil and boil 5 min. Cool. Combine syrup with lemon juice mixture. To serve, dilute lemonade syrup with equal parts cold water. Serve over ice.

Serves 15-20.

Grape cranberry lemonade

4 c. (1 qt.) grape cranberry drink
1 can (6 oz.) frozen lemonade concentrate
2 c. water

In a large pitcher, mix together grape cranberry drink, lemonade concentrate and water. Stir.

Serves 10-12.

Cranberry citrus punch

2 qt. cranberry juice cocktail, chilled
1 can (12 oz.) frozen pink lemonade concentrate, thawed
1 can (6 oz.) frozen orange juice concentrate, thawed
4 c. cold water
1 qt. ginger ale, chilled

In a large punch bowl mix cranberry juice cocktail, lemonade concentrate, orange juice concentrate, and water. Just before serving add ginger ale. Garnish with lemon and orange slices.

Serves 25-30.

Papaya-mango cocktail

This cocktail, high in digestive enzymes, is known as an antidote to over-eating and is served at Christmas in some of the leeward islands of the Caribbean.

1 part papaya juice
1 part mango juice
1 part lemon or lime juice
honey to taste
cherries to decorate

Mix all juices, preferably in an electric blender. Sweeten with honey to taste, blend again and chill slightly. Serve each glass decorated with a cherry on a stick.

Ruby cooler

4 c. (1 qt.) cranberry apple drink
4 t. instant tea
lemon wedges

In a large pitcher, mix together cranberry apple drink and tea. Pour over ice into tall glasses. Garnish with lemon wedges.

Serves 6.

Citrus delight

2 c. grapefruit juice
½ c. orange juice
¼ t. almond extract

Mix ingredients in pitcher, serve cold or with ice cubes.

Serves 3.

Runners welcome

After a hot run or long jog, fruit juice is almost too concentrated and acidic for the stomach. Runners find this a great thirst quencher and energy replacer, especially in summer.

1 part juice, orange, grapefruit, apple, grape, cranberry, nectar 1 part club soda or seltzer	Mix together in tall glass just before serving.

Seabreeze spritzer

½ c. lemon flavored iced tea mix 1 qt. grapefruit juice 1 c. club soda, chilled	In large pitcher, combine all ingredients except soda. Just before serving, add soda. Serve with ice and garnish, if desired, with lemon slices. Serves 6.

Cranberry fruit spritzer

4 oz. cranberry apple drink 2 oz. white grape juice club soda	In a large wine glass pour cranberry apple drink and white grape juice over ice. Add a splash of club soda. Garnish with grapes or a lime slice. Serves 1.

Cranberry collins

4 oz. cranberry apple drink
1 t. sweetened lime juice
club soda

In a tall glass, pour cranberry juice cocktail and lime juice over ice cubes. Top with club soda. Stir.

Serves 1.

Slippery run

3 c. cranberry apple drink
1 cinnamon stick
dash ground ginger
2 t. honey
2 tea bags

In a saucepan, heat cranberry juice cocktail, cinnamon stick, ginger, and honey just to boiling. Remove from heat and add tea bags. Cover, let stand 5 min. Remove tea bags and cinnamon stick. Pour into mugs and serve hot with orange slices and cinnamon sticks.

Serves 4.

Cranberry glögg

4 c. (1 qt.) cranberry juice cocktail
½ c. raisins
4 slices orange (stuck with two whole cloves each)
½ t. ground cardamon
½ t. ground cinnamon

In a large saucepan, mix together cranberry juice cocktail, raisins, orange slices and spices. Let stand several hours to blend flavors. When ready to serve, bring to a boil, lower heat and simmer 30 min. Serve in mugs with raisins and orange slices; serve with spoons.

Serves 6.

Red rooster

4 c. (1 qt.) cranberry apple drink
1 can (6 oz.) frozen lemonade concentrate

In a freezer container, mix together cranberry apple drink and lemonade concentrate. Freeze to an icy slush (about 3 hours). Spoon into glasses. Serve with short straws.

Serves 8.

Sea breeze

½ c. cranberry juice
½ c. grapefruit juice

Pour over ice into a tall glass. Garnish with slice of lime.

Serves 1.

Scarlet daiquiri

4 oz. cranberry juice cocktail
8 fresh or frozen whole strawberries
1 T. sugar
1 T. lime juice

In a blender or food processor container, process cranberry juice cocktail, strawberries, sugar, and lime juice until blended. Serve over crushed ice.

Serves 1.

Cape codder

3 oz. cranberry juice cocktail
1 t. lemon juice

Pour over ice in a tall glass. Stir.

Serves 1.

Carrot-pineapple appetizer

2 c. unsweetened pineapple juice
½ c. diced raw carrot
1 T. lemon juice
1 T. brewer's yeast
⅛ t. basil

Put all ingredients in an electric blender and blend until smooth.

Serves 4-6.

Morning pickup

½ c. unsweetened prune juice
½ c. fresh apple juice
1 t. wheat germ
1 t. yogurt
1 t. sesame oil

Blend all ingredients in an electric blender.

Serves 1.

Cranberry fruit pops

1 can (8 oz.) crushed pineapple
2 c. cranberry apple drink
1 c. strawberry or raspberry flavored yogurt

In a blender container, process crushed pineapple until smooth, add cranberry apple drink and yogurt, process until completely blended. Pour into two ice cube trays. Freeze about one hour until partially firm. Place wooden stick in center of each cube. Freeze until hard.

Serves 7-9.

Cranberry grapefruit punch

1 gal. cranberry juice cocktail
2 qt. grapefruit juice
1 can (6 oz.) frozen lemonade concentrate, thawed
1 bottle (28 oz.) club soda or seltzer

In a large punch bowl, mix cranberry juice cocktail, grapefruit juice, and lemonade concentrate. Chill. Just before serving, add club soda.

Serves 40-50.

Pink grapefruit fruit punch

4 c. pink grapefruit juice cocktail, chilled
4 c. unsweetened pineapple juice, chilled
2 c. white grape juice, chilled

In a punch bowl or large pitcher mix together pink grapefruit juice cocktail, pineapple juice, and white grape juice. Serve over ice.

Serves 10-15.

Cranberry wassail

1 gal. cranberry juice cocktail
5 c. apple juice
⅔ c. sugar
4 (3-in.) cinnamon sticks
2 t. whole allspice
1 med. orange, sliced
20 whole cloves

In a large sauce pot over medium heat, mix together cranberry juice cocktail, apple juice, sugar, cinnamon sticks, and allspice. Heat to boiling, reduce heat, and simmer 10 min. Strain punch to remove spices. Serve warm in a heat proof punch bowl or chill and serve over ice. For a more spirited punch, garnish with orange slices studded with cloves.

Serves 30-40.

Sand trap

1 pkg. (10 oz.) frozen raspberries, packed in syrup
4 c. (1 qt.) grapefruit juice

Cut frozen raspberries into six pieces. In a blender container, process frozen raspberries and grapefruit juice until blended. Pour into tall glasses over crushed ice.

Serves 8.

Pineapple-coconut health drink

½ c. coconut milk
½ c. unsweetened pineapple juice
1 t. wheat germ
1 T. yogurt

Combine all ingredients in an electric blender and blend until smooth.

Serves 1.

Fruit juice surprise

A nutritious variation on a breakfast fruit cup.

3 c. unsweetened fruit juice (grape, pineapple, apple, or orange)
1 c. mixed fruit pieces (apple, banana, melon, berry or orange)

Cut up fruit. Put some fruit in each glass; add juice.

Serves 4.

Batidos

A batido, meaning beaten, is a Spanish drink from the Carribean. It is a refreshing summertime delight.

1 c. chopped fruit (melon, mango, strawberries, pineapple, papaya, etc.)
½ c. ice cubes
¼ c. cold milk (or light cream)
confectioners' sugar to taste

Whip ingredients at high speed in blender and pour into chilled glass. Garnish, if desired, with shredded coconut.

Serves 1.

Fruit smoothie

2 c. pineapple, papaya or orange juice
1 c. cracked ice
1 c. melon, strawberries, pineapple chunks

Place all ingredients in blender and whip for 3 min.

Variation. Use fruit sherbet in place of ice.

Serves 4.

Watermelon juice

Force ripe watermelon through a very fine conical strainer. Cantaloupe juice can be made the same way. Served with ice, this is a refreshing hot weather drink. Melon juice can be blended with banana, peaches, or other soft fruit for a delicious "smoothie" shake (with or without ice cream). Melon juice also makes a good basis for summertime punches.

Easy blender lunch

1 banana
1 apple, cored
1 pear, cored
½ to ¾ c. orange juice
2 T. raisins

Place all ingredients in an electric blender and blend until smooth. Pour into a bowl and eat with a spoon, or drink from a glass.

Serves 1-2.

Pink banana whirl

2 c. cranapple juice
2 c. orange juice
1 ripe banana

Whirl in blender for 30 seconds. Serve in tall glasses.

Serves 3-4.

Apricot appetizer

2 c. unsweetened apricot nectar
½ c. brewer's yeast, optional
⅛ t. mace
1 sprig mint

Combine all the ingredients in an electric blender and blend until smooth.

Serves 4-6.

Rosy lemon quencher

¼ c. lemon flavored instant tea powder
2 T. sugar
2 c. cranberry juice cocktail
2 c. pineapple juice

In pitcher, mix lemon flavored instant tea powder with sugar. Stir in juices. Serve with ice and garnish, if desired, with lemon slices.

Serves 4.

Party punch

sherbet ring
1 pt. lemon sherbet
1 pt. lime sherbet

punch
1 can (1 qt., 14 oz.) orange-grapefruit juice, chilled
1 can (1 qt., 14 oz.) pineapple juice, chilled
1 can (12 oz.) apricot nectar, chilled
¼ c. sugar
1 qt. ginger ale, chilled

For sherbet ring, alternate scoops of lemon and lime sherbet in a 4½ cup ring mold; pack lightly. Freeze until firm. To unmold, dip mold in warm water just to the rim a few seconds. Invert onto a flat plate and slide into punch bowl.

For punch, combine orange-grapefruit juice, pineapple juice, apricot nectar and sugar in a punch bowl. Add ginger ale. Unmold sherbet ring into punch. Serve immediately.

Serves 6.

Christmas wassail

2 qt. apple cider
2 c. orange juice
1 c. lemon juice
1½ c. pineapple juice
4-6 whole cloves
sugar or honey to taste

Combine ingredients and bring to a simmer. Strain. Serve hot. Nice and decorative wih clove-studded oranges added to punch bowl.

Serves 12.

Frui-tea party punch

¾ c. instant tea powder
1 qt. cranberry juice cocktail, chilled
1 qt. water
2 cans (6 oz.) frozen orange juice concentrate
1 can (6 oz.) frozen lemonade concentrate
1 bottle (28 oz.) ginger ale, chilled
2 cups (1 pt.) lemon sherbet

In punch bowl, combine instant tea powder, cranberry juice, water and concentrates. Just before serving, add ginger ale and top with scoops of sherbet. Serve with ice and garnish, if desired, with lemon slices.

Serves 10-20.

Fantasia fruit punch

¾ c. lemon flavored iced tea mix
1 qt. water
1 can (6 oz.) can frozen orange juice concentrate
1 can (6 oz.) can frozen pineapple juice concentrate
suggested fresh fruits*
1 bottle (28 oz.) club soda, chilled

In punch bowl, combine lemon flavored iced tea mix, water, concentrates and suggested fresh fruits. Just before serving, add club soda. Serve with ice.
*Suggested fresh fruits—use any combination of the following to equal 5 cups: sliced strawberries, chopped apple or pear, melon balls, blueberries, raspberries or pineapple.

Variations: Substitute a 28 ounce bottle chilled ginger ale for club soda.

Serves 10-20.

Fruit juice popsicles

This is a nutritious and inexpensive way to make your own popsicles at home. Used as ice cubes, the juice is a delicious addition to iced tea or punch.

1 can frozen juice concentrate (grape, apple, orange, grapefruit, etc.)
2 cans water

Combine concentrate and water and pour into popsicle molds or into ice cube trays. Fill one tray with two cups liquid. Freeze until hard.

Serves 3-4.

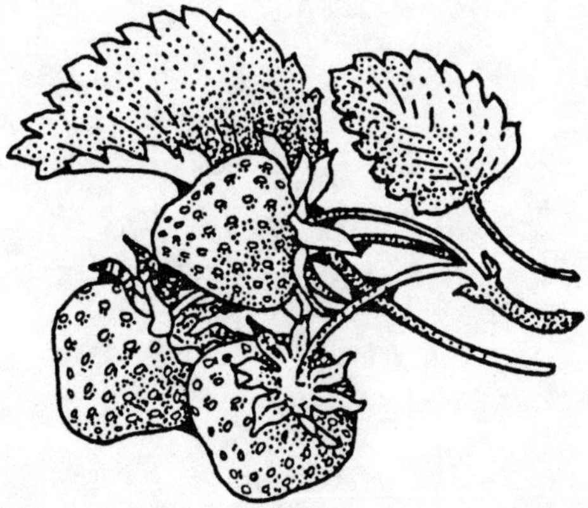

Vegetable juices

Vegetable juices

This is the shortest chapter in our beverage book. It is short on recipes not because we don't feel vegetable juice is important,but because you usually only find tomato juice in the store. Carrot juice is sometimes canned, but nearly all vitamins have been lost in the canning process. Nearly all vegetable juices must be served fresh, and therefore require a juice extractor. At one time one could only get fresh juice in a health food store, and to buy an extractor was an expensive proposition.

Today, however, extractors are within reason (around $65-$75 in most department stores). Krups, Oster and Braun are three reliable companies which sell excellent models. We highly recommend the addition of a juice extractor to your kitchen arsenal. Not only can you benefit by fresh juice from the hard cellulose vegetables like carrots, beets, celery, cabbage, green beans and green leafys, you can also juice whole tomatoes without skinning them and make cider when apples are plentiful and cheap. Many people do not care for vegetables in their diet—a sorry lack in our great American tastes. Infants to age three and many older people cannot digest a lot of cellulose and fiber. They can all benefit from the nutritional vegetable juices available with an extractor.

When you use your juicer, don't peel the vegetables as many vitamins and nutrients are contained in the skin. Wash all vegetables thoroughly, however. Carrot and beet tops are as nutritious their roots. The stalks of parsley, and celery bottoms, too, can be used. Little is wasted with an extractor.

Remember to use fresh vegetables when extracting juice. Vitamins, minerals and flavor are lost as the vegetables sit in the refrigerator. An ecological note: if you live in the country, the pulp can be mulched into gardens or fed to farm animals whose diet consists of cellulose.

Mixed vegetable juice

fresh tomatoes
carrots, plus tops if available
beets
onion, if desired
parsley
celery
watercress or spinach
green beans
cabbage

Combine varying amounts of these vegetables and process through a juice extractor. The majority of the juice will come from the tomatoes and carrots, with smaller amounts from the other vegetables serving to add distinctive flavors. Depending what is in season and inexpensive, include that in your recipe. Try adding fresh basil or oregano if available. Serve cold. Salt to taste before serving.

Carroty milk delight

½ c. carrot juice
½ c. milk
1 T. chopped almonds
dash cinnamon

Blend ingredients at high speed until frothy. Serve over ice cubes.

Serves 2.

Mock borscht

1 can beets, whole or sliced
1 c. yogurt
1 T. vinegar
1 small onion, peeled
salt, pepper to taste

Blend ingredients until smooth in blender. Serve chilled in glasses topped by a dollop of sour cream or yogurt.

Serves 2.

Minted yogurt soup

1½ c. peeled cucumbers (seeded if desired)
3 scallions with tops
3 T. fresh mint leaves
2 T. white vinegar
2 c. plain yogurt
salt, pepper to taste.

Blend ingredients at high speed for 2 min. Chill before serving in old-fashioned glasses or cups. Thin with a bit of water if desired. Garnish with mint sprig.

Serves 4.

Cold cucumber soup

1 med. onion
1 can cream of chicken or cream of mushroom soup
1 c. yogurt
¾ c. chicken stock
1 med. cucumber, peeled
⅛ t. celery salt or 1 sprig celery tops or parsley
⅛ t. curry powder
Tabasco sauce to taste
Worcestershire sauce to taste.

Combine ingredients in blender, blend until smooth. Adjust flavorings to individual taste. Chill before serving. Serve in glasses or soup bowls with thinly sliced cucumber and paprika to garnish.

Serves 4.

Carrot fizz

1 c. freshly extracted carrot juice
½ c. club soda
lemon juice to taste

Combine ingredients in a cold glass. Garnish with a dash of nutmeg.

Serves 1.

Refreshing tomato soup

1 c. tomato juice
1 c. buttermilk
dash basil leaves,
marjoram or thyme

Mix ingredients in tall glass or whir in blender 1 min. Serve cold.

Variation: Any freshly extracted vegetable juice can be substituted for tomato juice. The combination of juice and buttermilk is surprisingly refreshing.

Serves 1.

Liver cocktail

2 oz. raw calves' liver
1 carrot, quartered
dash salt
1 c. tomato juice
dash Worcestershire
sauce

Place the liver, carrot and salt in an electric blender and blend until smooth. Blend in tomato juice and Worcestershire sauce.

Serves 1.

Carrot pineapple combo

1 c. unsweetened
pineapple juice
1 c. fresh carrot juice
1 T. lemon juice
⅛ t. basil

Blend at high speed until frothy. Serve in chilled glasses.

Serves 2.

Tomato-sauerkraut drink

½ c. tomato juice
½ c. sauerkraut juice
1 t. chopped parsley
2 t. brewer's yeast
dash Worcestershire sauce
dash Tabasco

Blend all ingredients in an electric blender.

Serves 1.

Health cocktail

1 qt. skinned and cored ripe tomatoes
1 large sprig parsley
1 t. finely chopped scallion
2 T. chopped inner-rib celery leaves
1 t. salt

Put the tomatoes in an electric blender, one at a time, and blend until smooth after each addition. Add remaining ingredients; blend until smooth. Serve very cold. You can use 3 cups canned tomatoes if fresh ones are not available. To skin tomatoes easily, immerse them in gently boiling or scalding water for 1 min. The pierced skin will slip off.

Serves 3.

Vegetable drink

½ c. tomato juice
¼ c. celery juice
¼ c. carrot juice
¼ bunch watercress, chopped
1 t. chopped parsley
1 t. lemon juice
2 t. brewer's yeast

Blend all ingredients in an electric blender.

Serves 2

Tea and tea-based drinks

Tea and tea-based drinks

According to official sources, tea is the world's second most popular drink; water is the first! Chinese legend says that 5000 years ago the great emperor Shen-Nung demanded water be boiled before drinking for health purposes. Tea leaves accidentally fell into the boiling water, the emperor enjoyed the aroma, sampled the result. The rest is history.

Tea drinking came to the western world during the 1600s and became a big industry in the 1800s—the time of clipper ships. In the early 1900s, Thomas Sullivan, a New York tea wholesaler, tried selling smaller amounts of tea in silk bags instead of in larger tins. People started brewing the tea right in the bag. And you know that result. The most recent tea improvement is our modern instant tea powder.

Tea is an evergreen that belongs to the Camellia family. In the wild it grows into a bush thirty feet high. It grows only in certain climate-right regions—parts of China, India, Indonesia, eastern Africa and South America. Actually, there are only three different types of tea: black, green and oolong. They come from the same tea bushes. Black tea is treated in a fermenting process which turns the leaves black and produces a hearty brew. Green tea is not fermented and oolong is a compromise between black and green tea, semi-fermented.

There are over 3,000 varieties of teas, whether black, green or oolong. Where it is grown, what kind of soil it is grown in, what kind of aromatic herbs and barks the leaves are cured with—produces a tea with distinctive qualities. Some of the kinds of tea you may encounter are Assam, Ceylon, Darjeeling, Formosa Oolong, Jasmine, Keemun, and Lapsang Souchong. Ninety-seven percent of the tea drunk in America is of the black variety. We recommend trying many different kinds, deciding for yourself which is your personal favorite.

The word "pekoe" is not a type of tea. This refers to the size of leaf as do the words Orange Pekoe, Souchong, Broken Pekoe, Fannings and Fines. Incidentally, the tea "dust" which is left at the bottom of the chests and after processing is what is found in tea bags. Experts generally agree that loose tea is preferable in taste to the tea in bags. Perhaps not as convenient, though.

Technically, tea refers only to the plant we have been discussing, but herbal teas have gained enormous popularity in our time. Many are held to have medicinal properties: They alleviate colds, hasten sleep, cure gout, etc. We recommend trying herbal teas because many of them taste so good. There is a large variety: catnip, mint, strawberry leaf, comfrey, bancha, camomile, alfalfa leaf, rosehip, to name a few. Virtually any aromatic plant can be made into a tea drink.

For those who do not want the caffein in regular tea, we recommend trying these herbal alternatives. They are delicious cold, iced with fruit juice, garnished with lemon or orange. When aromatic plants are in season, you can harvest them, wash them thoroughly and dry them, keeping the leaves for your own homemade herbal tea supply.

We must speak a bit of the proper way to brew tea, not because it is a ritual, but because practical things bring out the best possible tea flavor in brewing.

1. Use freshly drawn *cold* water, or bottled water. The better the water the better the tea. Water is best when it is aerated (full of oxygen), and will bring out the full character of tea. Hot water from the tap is generally stale from standing in water heater pipes.
2. Bring the water to a full, rolling boil and pour it onto the tea immediately. If the water is not boiling the tea will not brew properly. If the water is boiled for too long, or boiled twice, it loses its aeration and results in flat tasting tea.
3. Preheat the teapot by filling it with very hot water and letting it stand until time to make the tea. Empty the pot and add tea and boiling water. Cover the pot during brewing time so the water is kept hot. If you brew by the cup, cover the cup with a saucer.
4. Brew for three-five minutes only. If left too long, the tea will turn bitter by releasing too much of its tannin. Go by the clock not by the color: Some teas are light and some dark. Remove the tea bags or the infusion ball or tea leaves. Squeeze the bags of their liquid, press the loose leaves with the back of a spoon. The leaves absorb seven times their weight in water and contain delicious tea.
5. Use one teaspoon of loose tea or one teabag per cup of water.
6. Lemon and sugar complement tea's delicate flavor best. Most experts generally advise against cream with tea as the oiliness hides the full flavor of tea. Milk is better than cream.

Iced tea was created in 1904 at the St. Louis World's Fair. No one was buying hot tea from an Indian tea merchant because of the sweltering heat. The merchant poured the brew over ice and created an instant success.

We recommend cooling tea before pouring it over ice since hot tea melts the ice and dilutes the flavor too much. Let the tea cool at room temperature, it tends to cloud up when refrigerated. The flavor isn't affected by this cloudiness; the cloudiness is the solid particles suspended in the tea water. You can clear this cloudiness sometimes by adding a little boiling water.

There are two cold water brewing methods for delicious iced tea. Try six teabags in a quart of water and refrigerating overnight. Remove teabags and pour over ice. Sun tea is the latest hotweather popular to make iced tea. In a gallon jar of water put eight-ten regular tea bags. Cover and place in a sunny window or in sunshine for three-four hours. Refrigerate after five hours of brewing. Remove teabags. This tea will not cloud up as readily. Always use glass containers with tea, as metal sometimes interferes with the delicate flavor.

Tempting tea-light

1½ c. boiling water
6 tea bags
¼ c. sugar
3 c. apple juice, chilled
2 (12 oz.) cans ginger ale, chilled
vanilla ice cream

In teapot, pour boiling water over tea bags; cover and brew 5 min. Remove tea bags; stir in sugar and cool. In large pitcher, combine tea and juice. Just before serving, add ginger ale and top with ice cream.

Serves 8.

Citrus tea punch

½ c. sugar syrup
1 c. cold tea
½ c. pineapple juice
1 c. orange juice
1½ c. water
½ c. lemon or lime juice

Make sugar syrup with ½ cup water and ½ cup sugar; heat water to near-boiling and dissolve sugar. Let cool. Mix all ingredients together, chill and serve.

Serves 4.

Tropical tea cup

2½ c. water
4 orange-spice flavor tea bags
1 can (8 oz.) sliced pineapple in natural juice, drained (reserve juice)
3 T. sugar
flaked coconut

In medium saucepan, bring water to a boil. Add orange-spice flavor tea bags; cover and brew 5 min. Remove tea bags. Stir in reserved juice and sugar; heat through. Just before serving, top with pineapple and coconut.

Serves 4.

Lime delight

3 T. instant tea powder
½ c. sugar
1 qt. water
¼ c. lime juice

In large pitcher, mix instant tea powder with sugar. Stir in water and lime juice. Serve with ice and garnish, if desired, with lime slices and maraschino cherries.

Serves 4.

Russian fruit tea

1 c. hot, brewed black or herb tea
raw sugar or honey to taste
1 apple, quartered, cored and finely diced

Sweeten the tea with sugar or honey and add the apple. Let stand several minutes then eat the apple pieces with a spoon and drink the tea.

Note: Other fruits, such as pears, peaches, oranges and grapes can be substituted for the apple.

Serves 1.

Early morning eye opener

1 c. boiling water
5 orange herbal tea bags
¼ c. honey
1 c. (½ pt.) whipping or heavy cream
2 eggs
1½ c. ice cubes (about 9 to 11)

In teapot, pour boiling water over orange herbal tea bags; cover and brew 5 min. Remove tea bags; stir in honey and cool.

In blender, combine tea, cream and eggs; process at high speed until blended. Add ice cubes, one at a time; process at high speed until blended. Garnish, if desired, with orange slices.

Serves 4.

Constant comment tea

2 T. orange peel, diced and dried
2 T. lemon leaves, diced and dried
8-10 whole cloves
1 T. cinnamon
¾ c. tea leaves

Dry the orange peel and lemon leaves in low oven. Mix all ingredients together. When preparing tea, steep for 3-5 min., to attain full flavor.

Tea punch

2 c. sugar
3 c. strong tea
juice of 2 lemons
juice of 6 oranges
9 c. water
2 cans ginger ale

Mix together all ingredients except ginger ale. Chill. Add chilled ginger ale just before serving. Add mint for pleasing garnish and flavor.

Serves 16.

Fruit 'n tea punch

3 c. water
3 T. loose, black tea (6 tea bags)
2½ c. sugar
2 c. lemon juice
1 qt. orange juice
1 qt. plus 1 c. pineapple juice
3 qts. cold water

Heat water to a hard boil; pour over tea. Cover container and steep for 3 min. Strain. Add sugar; stir until dissolved. Chill thoroughly. Combine juices and water with chilled tea solution. Cover and place in refrigerator to chill thoroughly before serving. Note: Grape juice may be substituted for pineapple juice.

Serves 25.

Instant spiced tea

½ c. instant tea powder 1 t. grated lemon rind 2 c. orange juice powdered concentrate 2 c. sugar 1 t. cloves 1 t. allspice ¼ t. ginger	Blend together all ingredients. Store in an air-tight container. Use 2 teaspoons per cup of boiling water. Use the same proportions for iced tea.

Instant spiced tea

2 c. instant tea powder 2 c. orange juice powder concentrate 1 c. sugar 1 t. cinnamon ½ t. ground cloves	Combine ingredients and keep in an airtight container. Add 2 teaspoons mixture to 1 cup hot water. Use the same proportions for iced tea.

Common cold soother

4 c. hot tea juice of 1 lemon honey to taste	Mix all ingredients together, then pour into mugs. Serve with a grain of salt. Serves 4.

Citrus peel tea

This is an ideal tea if you have a surplus or oranges, lemons, limes or grapefruit and want to utilize the peel. The tea is a wonderful winter warm-up and a marvelous base for cold punches or wassail bowls.

1 c. dried citrus peel
6 c. boiling water

Dry citrus peel in sun. Add peel to boiling water and allow to steep until the desired strength is achieved. If desired, add a stick of cinnamon or several whole cloves while steeping for a spicy variation.

Serves 6.

Lemon leaf tea

If you live where you are able to get fresh lemon leaves, here is a zesty and refreshing tea, hot or iced.

2 c. lemon leaves
8 c. boiling water

Add washed leaves to boiling water and allow to steep until the desired strength is achieved, about 5 min. Serve hot or iced with lemon wedges as garnish. Sweeten to taste.

Serves 8.

Indian spice tea

This spicy tea is a great complement, hot or iced, to Indian cuisine.

5 c. boiling water
2 peppercorns
4 sticks cinnamon
2 cardamon seeds
4 bay leaves
4 whole cloves

Add ingredients to boiling water for 5 min., then let steep for another 5 min. Serve hot or iced. Sweeten if desired.

Serves 4.

We include a couple of easy and delicious cocoa recipes for those chilly times.

Hot cinnamon cocoa

4 T. sugar
4 T. cocoa
½ t. cinnamon
dash salt
⅓ c. water
4 c. milk
¼ t. vanilla

Mix sugar, cocoa, cinnamon, salt and water together in a 2 quart sauce pan. Heat quickly to a boil; lower heat; cook for 3 min. Stir in milk and vanilla. Keep hot but don't boil.

Serves 4.

Hot cocoa

1 T. cocoa
2 T. sugar
2 c. water
⅔ c. instant nonfat *dry milk*
¼ t. vanilla

Mix cocoa, sugar, and ⅓ cup of the water in a pan. Heat to boiling and cook slowly for 5 min. to make cocoa syrup. Remove cocoa syrup from heat. Add rest of water. Then add *dry* milk. Stir or beat until smooth. Heat but do not boil. Add vanilla.

Serves 2.

Coffee and coffee-based drinks

Coffee and coffee-based drinks

As the popular song of the '40s says: "Coffee and tea and Java and me, a sip, a sip, a sip, a sip, a ahhhh!" Coffee may well be the national drink of America; certainly the aroma of freshly brewed coffee, its taste and exhilarating fatigue-allaying qualities go deep in our consciences. Coffee has been around since 1668 but it wasn't until the Boston Tea Party and the resulting tea embargo that we took to coffee in a big way.

Coffee comes from Arabia originally, and was shipped from the port of Mocha (hence the name.) It is now grown in many hot, moist countries where there is a lot of rainfall: Indonesia (hence the name Java), South America (Colombian), and Africa among them.

A coffee tree lives at least 30 years, and is an evergreen shrub belonging to the madder family. The beans are the seeds from the fragrant white flower. Beans are red when ripe. They are picked by hand, dried and then roasted. The growing region, the soil, the method and length of roasting are all factors giving the different tastes to coffee. Very often the beans are blended before grinding, each type and roast adding its uniqueness to the final taste.

Each country drinks coffee in a slightly different way. The Turks powder the beans finely and sweeten the brew heavily. They do not strain the coffee but let the coffee settle in the bottom of the cup. The Italians roast the beans until very dark, almost charred, and make their marvelous espresso, heavy and smoky. In France, most people prefer *cafe au lait*: half coffee, half hot scalded milk. In Austria, coffee with whipped cream and often the addition of chocolate or cocoa is popular. Americans prefer clear coffee.

No one agrees on the best way to brew the perfect cup. Espresso and Turkish coffee require special machines. In America we have percolators, drip, and now, machines which heat the water and drip it into the ground beans.

These new machines take much of the guess work out of coffee making and are thought to be preferable to percolators. (Metal containers are losing favor in coffee making, since glass is easier to clean, and coffee picks up tastes easily.)

Coffee makers do agree on several things necessary to make a good cup of coffee. We list those things and hope they help you toward a better cup of coffee.

Coffee. Beans should be stored in an air-tight container in a dark cool place (preferably the refrigerator), and ground fresh before brewing. What gives coffee its wonderful taste is the oil in the bean. This is released when the bean is ground and then infused into the water when the boiling water passes through the grinds. When the bean is ground and exposed too long to the air, the oil goes stale, loses its aroma, and turns rancid.

If you grind your own beans, grind only enough for the pot you are making. Don't run the grinder at high speed for a long time, but activate it in spurts. This keeps the blades from getting overheated and "cooking" the oils being released from the beans.

If you buy ready-ground coffee, keep the tin refrigerated, or even in the freezer section. If you have an entire pound ground at the store, transfer it to an air-tight tin and refrigerate.

Amount. For American coffee, the standard measure is one heaping tablespoon of grinds for every six ounce cup of coffee. If you are making only one or two cups of coffee you will have to use more grinds; if you are making a full pot, you can use slightly less. A good rule to remember is "one spoonful for the pot" when measuring out grinds. If you use the drip method, stir the finished coffee before pouring as more infusing happens at the beginning and the stronger coffee is at the bottom.

Water. Use only fresh, cold water from the tap or bottle. This will be aerated and gives a much pleasanter taste to the coffee. Don't worry about the chlorination in your water affecting the coffee's taste. Chlorine is released from the water upon boiling.

If using the drip method, bring the water to a boil and turn off. Use within a couple of minutes. Don't overboil the water.

Reheating. Have you noticed how delicate and fresh that first cup of coffee is and how much less tasty the second becomes? This is because most home and commercial coffee machines have heated coils to keep the pot warm. This is all wrong as the essential oils released from the coffee bean continue to cook over heat and this changes the taste of the coffee. At last we have become savvy about this, and stores are now selling vacuum pitchers in their coffee sections. Invest in one. As soon as your coffee is made, pour it into the pitcher and screw on the lid. The coffee you don't use immediately keeps hot all day. You can have a fresh cup with dinner if you like!

Incidentally, we recommend pouring leftover coffee into ice cube trays and freezing. These make ideal cubes when you want iced coffee, keeping the brew strong and pure.

Cleaning. A neglected part of coffee making is making sure all utensils are free from oil residue from previous brews. As with all oils, coffee oil adheres to surfaces and becomes stale. This always affects subsequent batches. Glass items clean the best, and soap and water are usually effective on these. Metal containers need commercial coffee cleaning powders occasionally, or a good scour with baking soda. Fill pots with very hot water and add several tablespoons of soda and let stand for half an hour. This helps remove old oil from walls and bottom of pot.

Instant coffee. This is the poor or hasty man's coffee and has little similarity to freshly brewed. Ever. Instant coffee is effective in cooking, however, when the taste of coffee is needed. You can also come closer to real coffee taste with instant if you pour boiling water over the powder, then bring the coffee to a boil over a flame before serving.

Old fashioned egg coffee

Scandinavians take special pride in making coffee this old-fashioned way; campers find it convenient. The clarifying effect of the egg white helps the coffee to sparkle.

4½ qt. water
1½ c. regular grind coffee
1 egg
½ c. cold water

In large saucepan, saucepot or big coffee pot, bring 4½ quarts water to boil. Combine coffee and egg, reserving shell. Stir coffee-egg mixture and shell into boiling water. Return to boil.

Remove from heat and let stand 2 min. Slowly pour in cold water to help settle grounds. Strain, if desired.

Serves 8-11.

Spicy coffee

4 serving-measure of ground coffee
4 c. cold water
⅛ t. cinnammon or
⅛ t. cloves or
⅛ t. nutmeg or
1 t. cocoa or
1½ t. brown sugar or
1 t. molasses
⅛ t. ginger

Add whichever spice you desire to your coffee for a different taste. Perk or drip as usual. Serve hot with milk or cream.

Serves 4.

Belgian coffee

1 egg white
¼ t. vanilla
½ c. heavy cream
hot coffee
sugar to taste

Beat egg white stiff. Add vanilla to heavy cream and whip. Combine with egg white. Fill coffee cups ⅓ full with cream mixture. Fill with hot coffee. Serve at once. Sweeten to taste.

Serves 4.

Caffè Borgia

Italian coffee
hot chocolate
sweetened whipped cream
grated orange peel

Combine equal quantities of steaming Italian coffee and hot chocolate. Pour into cups and top with sweetened whipped cream. Sprinkle with grated orange peel.

Café au lait

This is one of the joys of breakfasting in France. Every breakfast tray bears this steaming favorite accompanied by flaky croissants. To prepare café au lait, you need two pots, one for the strong, hot coffee and one for an equal quantity of hot, rich milk. Pour simultaneously from both pots into cups.

Brazilian coffee-chocolate

2 (2 oz.) squares unsweetened chocolate
3 T. sugar
1 c. extra-strength hot coffee
3 c. milk
1 qt. coffee ice cream

In double boiler melt chocolate over hot water. Add sugar. Blend well. Add hot coffee slowly, while stirring. Scald milk. Combine with coffee mixture; cook over hot water 10 min. Remove from heat. Beat with rotary egg beater until frothy; chill thoroughly. Serve in tall glasses with large scoop of coffee ice cream.

Serves 5-6.

Caffè Cappucino

Italian coffee steamed milk cinnamon nutmeg sugar	Combine equal quantities of steaming Italian coffee and steaming milk. Pour into Cappuccino cups and sprinkle with cinnamon and nutmeg. Serve with sugar.

Café Mexicano

4 t. chocolate syrup ½ c. heavy cream ¾ t. cinnamon, divided ¼ t. nutmeg 1 T. sugar 1½ c. strong hot coffee	Put 1 teaspoon chocolate syrup into each of 4 small cups. Combine cream, ¼ teaspoon cinnamon, nutmeg and sugar. Whip. Stir remaining ½ teaspoon cinnamon into hot coffee. Pour coffee into cups. Stir to blend with syrup. Top with spiced whipped cream. Serves 4.

Romana espresso coffee

espresso coffee lemon peel	Fill tall, warm glasses with espresso coffee. Add twist of lemon peel. *Variation:* Pour espresso coffee over cracked ice, in tall glass, add simple syrup to taste (sugar dissolved in water). Garnish with lemon peel.

Coffee tropicale

1½ c. strong, cool coffee
cracked ice
1 T. granulated sugar

Fill electric blender container half full of finely chopped ice. Add coffee and sugar. Blend until thick and foamy. Pour into tall glasses. Serve with milk if desired.

Serves 4.

Spiced Vienna coffee

In romantic 19th century Vienna, dollops of whipped cream crowned one's coffee. One demanded the exact shade of coffee, created by the amount of whipped cream used.

3 c. very hot extra-strength coffee
2 cinnamon sticks
4 whole cloves
4 allspice berries.
whipped cream
nutmeg
sugar

Pour coffee over cinnamon sticks, cloves and allspice berries. Let stand over lowest heat for 10 to 15 min. Strain. Pour into table wine glasses and top with softly whipped cream. Sprinkle with nutmeg and serve with sugar.

Serves 6.

Viennese coffee frost

6 c. Italian, or double-strength coffee
4 cinnamon sticks, crushed
3 cloves
8 allspice berries
ice
sugar to taste
whipped cream

While coffee is still hot, pour over cinnamon, cloves and allspice berries. After an hour, strain the beverage and pour over ice in tall glasses. Sweeten to taste with simple sugar syrup and top with whipped cream.

Serves 4-6.

Creamed cinnamon coffee

4 c. extra-strength hot coffee
3 sticks cinnamon
sugar, or simple sugar syrup
½ c. heavy cream
ice

Pour hot coffee over cinnamon sticks and let stand for about 1 hour. Remove cinnamon sticks and sweeten coffee to taste. Add heavy cream and chill. Pour over cracked ice in tall glasses and use cinnamon sticks as stirrers.

Serves 4-5.

Coffee tropicana

4 c. cold extra strength coffee
1 t. rum flavoring
1 c. light cream
club soda or seltzer water
sugar to taste

Combine coffee, cream, flavoring and chill. Pour into 6 tall glasses, fill to tops with club soda. Stir gently and sweeten to individual tastes.

Serves 4.

Strawberry breeze

- 1 c. cold extra-strength coffee
- 1 c. crushed or chopped ice
- 1 c. milk
- 1 c. strawberries, fresh or frozen
- 2 T. sugar

Put ice in cup to half-cup level then fill to top with coffee. Combine with remaining ingredients in blender and whip at high speed until foamy. Serve in tall glasses.

Serves 4.

Spiced iced coffee

- 8 c. coffee
- 1 whole cinnamon stick
- 8 whole cloves
- sugar to taste
- cream

Brew 8 cups coffee using 1½ approved measures of coffee per cup. When coffee is brewed add cinnamon and cloves. Allow to cool then refrigerate until chilled. Put ice cubes in tall glasses and strain coffee over the ice. Pour cream into the coffee just before serving. Serve with sugar.

Serves 8.

Peanut butter café

- 1 c. cold strong coffee
- 1 c. milk
- 1 heaping T. peanut butter
- 4 T. sugar

Mix in blender at high speed until foamy. Serve in tall glasses.

Serves 2.

Mocha mocha

2½ c. cold strong coffee
cocoa
2 c. chocolate ice cream

Place all ingredients in bowl and blend with rotary beater or wire whip, or in blender until smooth. Pour into tall glasses.

Serves 4.

Coffee nog

1 c. cold strong coffee
1 c. milk
1 T. sugar
3 T. instant egg nog powder

Mix all ingredients in blender at high speed. Serve in egg nog cups.

Serves 2-3.

Brazilian coffee

1 c. strong coffee
1 square (1 oz.) unsweetened chocolate
¼ c. sugar
dash of salt
3 c. milk

Melt chocolate in coffee over low heat in 2-quart saucepan. Add sugar and salt; stir to dissolve. Gradually add milk, stirring contantly. Heat to serving. Beat with rotary beater until frothy. Serve hot, topped with a spoonful of whipped cream, if desired.

Serves 4.

Licorice stick

1½ qt. hot coffee
1 t. anise extract
sugar to taste

Combine coffee, anise extract and sugar to taste in serving pot. Stir thoroughly. Serve in cups or mugs.

Serves 6-8.

Greb's grog

peel from 1 orange
peel from 1 lemon
4 cinnamon sticks
1½ t. whole cloves
⅓ c. sugar
½ c. chocolate syrup
½ t. anise flavoring
2 qt. strong hot coffee
whipped cream

Combine the orange and lemon peels, cut in strips, with cinnamon sticks, cloves, sugar, chocolate syrup, anise flavoring and coffee in large carafe or deep chafing dish. Steep over very low heat for 15 min. (do not boil). Serve in demitasse or small mugs, with a twist of lemon peel and a spoonful of whipped cream.

Serves 8-10.

Mocha spiced

2 c. water
1 stick cinnamon
6 whole cloves
4 allspice berries
ground coffee
whipped cream
cocoa powder
vanilla extract

Boil water and spices for 10 min. Pour over drip coffee grinds for 3 servings coffee. Serve in mugs into which you have folded cocoa powder and vanilla flavoring. Top with whipped cream and sweeten, if desired.

Serves 3.

Spicy icy coffee

3 c. hot coffee
2 sticks cinnamon
4 cloves
4 allspice berries

Pour hot coffee over spices, let stand 1 hour. Pour strained coffee over ice in 4 tall glasses. Garnish with lemon peel. Sweeten, if desired.

Serves 4.

Continental fizz

1½ c. extra strong hot coffee
½ t. Angosturn bitters
½ t. vanilla
1½ T. sugar

Mix ingredients. Pour into 4 tall glasses. Add ice cubes. Fill glasses to top with club soda. Garnish rim with orange slice.

Serves 4.

Cardamom icy

Try this Middle Eastern flavor after a Greek or Turkish meal.

6 cardamom seeds or
⅛ t. cardamom powder
coffee

Boil seeds for 10 min. in water for 4 cups coffee. Strain into drip grinds or use in percolator with grinds to make 4 cups coffee. If cardamom powder is used, add directly to grinds in drip or perk method. After coffee is brewed, pour over ice in tall glasses. Garnish with pineapple tidbits and maraschino cherries. Sweeten, if desired.

Serves 4.

FREDERICK E. KAHN, M.D. is the general editor for the series of cookbooks to appear under the general title of "Preparing Food the Healthy Way."

Dr. Kahn, a practicing psychiatrist, brings to this series his interest and expertise in the essential nutritional and psychological aspects of personal health. In that vein, he is presently involved in a study of individuals who have suffered from Myocardial Infarction.

He is currently serving as an Assistant Attending Physician at both Columbia College of Physicians and Surgeons, and St. Luke's-Roosevelt Hospital in New York City, and is a member of the Harry Stack Sullivan Society of the William Alanson White Institute for Psychoanalysis.

He is a graduate of the University of Michigan and Wayne State University Medical School.

Index

PREPARING FOOD THE HEALTHY WAY SERIES

ORDER FORM

If you've enjoyed using this book, and would like copies of any other books in this series, indicate the *number of copies of each title* you wish to order, enclose a check or money order for the appropriate amount, and send in the entire page. Allow 6 weeks for delivery.

NUMBER OF COPIES

___ Appetizers
___ Beverages
___ Breads & Cakes
___ Breakfast & Brunch
___ Canning and Preserving
___ Chinese Food
___ Cooking With Kids
___ Dessert
___ Fish
___ Fruit

NUMBER OF COPIES

___ Ground Meat
___ International Meals
___ One-Dish Meals
___ Outdoor Cooking
___ Party Cooking
___ Poultry
___ Sandwiches
___ Sauces
___ Seafood

Please send me the books checked above. I have ordered ___ books at $4.95 each.

	NUMBER OF COPIES		PER COPY		
		X	$4.95	=	$
Plus postage and handling		X	.50	=	$
Total enclosed					$

Mail this form and your check to: Nautilus Communications, Inc., 460 East 79th Street, New York, NY 10021. No COD's, please!

Name ___

Address ___

City ___ State ___ Zip ___

Dear Reader:

We hope that you are enjoying this book, and that you have seen some of the other books in this series. If you would like to order additional titles, an order form is enclosed for your convenience.

Many of the recipes in this book have been provided by outside contributors. We are always looking for additional recipes and would welcome receiving your favorites for inclusion in future cookbooks.

If you would like to send us recipes, please use the form below. ***Recipes must be typed.*** *If your recipe is used, you will receive a free copy of the book in which it appears. If you need more forms, you may make photocopies of this one.*

Recipe name ______________________________

Ingredients

______________________ ______________________

______________________ ______________________

______________________ ______________________

______________________ ______________________

______________________ ______________________

______________________ ______________________

______________________ ______________________

Baking temperature ______________________

Directions ______________________________

____

____

____

Serving size ______________________ *List variations on back.*

Name ______________________________

Address ______________________________

City ____________ *State* ____________ *Zip* ____________

Send your recipes to:
Nautilus Communications, Inc.,
460 East 79th Street,
New York, NY 10021